James Galway

GOLDEN MOMENTS

10 Short Encores for Flute and Piano

Edited by

JAMES GALWAY

Piano Reduction by Phillip Moll

GREAT PERFORMER'S EDITION

ED 3977
ISBN 0-7935-5031-9

G. SCHIRMER, Inc.

DISTRIBUTED BY

 HAL•LEONARD®
CORPORATION

7777 W. BLUEMOUND RD. P.O. BOX 13819 MILWAUKEE, WI 53213

FOREWORD

One of the great attractions of the flute is its suitability for playing, with expression, color, and charm, melodies of every sort. Away from the intellectual and technical challenges of the concerto, sonata, and virtuoso showpiece repertoire, it is a pleasure for player and listener alike to enjoy a well-known tune. No recital we play would feel complete without a couple of these tunes as a way of saying thank you to the audience for coming and listening to our program.

The melodies in the following collection were originally composed for voice, piano, or violin, but they sound fine on the flute as well, so we have no compunctions about borrowing them. Play them with wit and warmth and they will, we hope, provide you and your listeners with many "golden moments" of enjoyment.

JAMES GALWAY AND PHILLIP MOLL

AVE MARIA

J.S. Bach
adapted by Charles Gounod *

Andante con moto

* Adapted from *The Well-Tempered Clavier*, Book 1, Prelude no. 1.

* At m. 17 and again at m. 19, Gounod indicates a *subito p* following the *crescendo* in the preceding measure. I prefer a gradual tapering to *piano.* —J. Galway

* Optional: piano part one octave higher until ** m. 39 (two measures from end).

MINUET IN G

Ludwig van Beethoven

Trio

Menuetto
D.C. al Fine

NOCTURNE IN C# MINOR

Frédéric Chopin

SALUT D'AMOUR

Edward Elgar

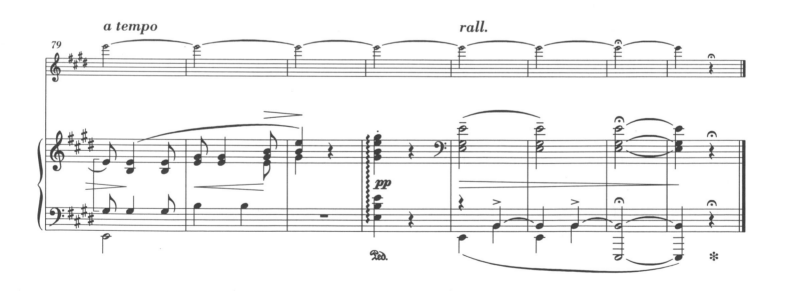

GAVOTTE

François-Joseph Gossec

Allegretto grazioso

SERENADE

Joseph Haydn

IRISH TUNE FROM COUNTY DERRY

Traditional

SPRING SONG
from *Songs Without Words*, op. 62 no. 6

Felix Mendelssohn

RONDO ALLA TURCA
from *Piano Sonata*, K. 331

Wolfgang Amadeus Mozart

Allegretto

SERENADE
(Ständchen)

Franz Schubert

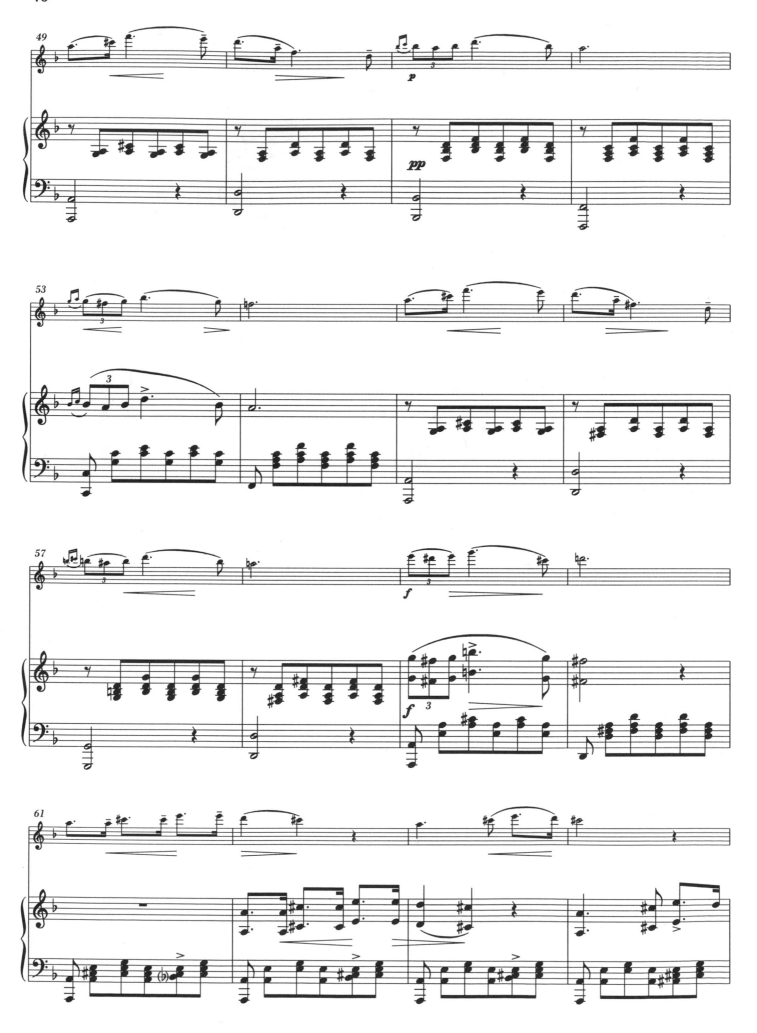